Here are some things you can do with my Laugh Out Loud joke book:

1. Read it out loud.
2. Read it to yourself.
3. When there's a wobbly chair, you can slip it under one the legs to stop it wobbling.
4. Line it up with some other books across the middle of a table so you can play table-tennis over it.
5. Learn some of the jokes so that you can tell them to other people.
6. Make it into a salad.
7. Lend it.
8. Try to get it back from the person you lent it to.
9. Pretend that you made up all the jokes yourself.
10. Cover it with brown paper and write on it: *'Great Expectations'* by *Charles Dickens*, and everyone will think you are very clever.

5

Q. What do you call a nose with no body?
A. Nobody knows.

Q. Why did the fly fly?
A. Because the spider spied 'er.

Q. How does Darth Vader like his toast?
A. On the dark side.

Q. What do you get if you cross an ape and a prawn?
A. A shrimpanzee.

6

HA HA!

The

LAUGH OUT LOUD

HEE HEE!

Joke Book

Illustrated by Sarah HORNE

Michael ROSEN

■ SCHOLASTIC

Introduction

I woke up one morning and thought, 'I wonder what was the first ever joke book?' I looked and looked and found that the oldest one we've got comes from Greece in the fourth century (that's sometime between the years 400 and 499!). It's written by two men, so perhaps they were a kind of 'double-act' like Ant and Dec.

Anyway, some 1,500 years later, I'm doing it too. But I'm not a double-act.

Q. Why's a frog with no legs not much fun to be with?
A. It's unhoppy.

Q. Why did the toilet think it was too hot?
A. It was flushed.

My dog doesn't feel too good.
How do you know?
I asked him.
What did you say?
How do you feel?
What did he say?
Ruff.

7

I know a guy who got a job mending a trampoline, but it fell through.

I know a guy who got a job making a cage: he couldn't get out of it.

I know a guy who mends lifts: it's a bit up and down.

I know a guy who got a job looking for water. Well, well, well.

I know a guy who had an accident when he went bungee jumping.

It's OK, he's bouncing back.

Q. What game do crocodiles like playing?
A. Swallow my leader.

Q. What's the longest word in the world?
A. Smiles – there's a mile between the two s's.

We were having a meal in a restaurant and the waiter gave us our vegetables. Amongst them was a single piece of sweetcorn.
'See that?' the waiter said, 'it should have a horn on it.'
'Why's that?' I asked.
'It's a unicorn,' he said.

Q. What did the nose know?
A. Only the nose knows.

Q. What do you get if you cross a kangaroo with an elephant?
A. Great big holes all over Australia.

Q. What did the queen bee say to the naughty bee?
A. Bee-hive yourself.

A penguin dived deep into the sea and came up again really fast.
It heard an animal nearby saying, 'Well done, penguin.'
The penguin wondered who it was and looked round.
It was a seal of approval.

I thought I ought to take a warm jumper with me. A bit of it was hanging out the side of my bag but most of it fitted in.
It was just in case.

Q. Who's like a female sheep round here?
A. Ewe.

12

Q. Why did the baker stop making bagels?
A. She got tired of the hole thing.

**Q. What do you get if you cross a
Diplodocus and a lemon?
A. A dino-sour.**

Q. Which dinosaur was pleased you met
him and his mates?
A. Aren't-you-glad-you-saurus.

**Q. Which country is always a bit on the
cold side?
A. Chile.**

Q. What's a pirate's favourite takeaway?
A. Fish and ships.

Q. What kind of snake cleans car windows?
A. A windscreen viper.

Q. What did one font say to the other?
A. You're just my type.

Q. What's the best side of the house to put a porch on?
A. The outside.

Q. Where do Santa's little helpers go when they're ill?
A. The elf centre.

Q. Why was the chef in the Greek
restaurant such a cheery guy?
A. He had a very good sense of hummus.

**The headteacher walked into the room
and a little girl was rude to him.
'I didn't come here to be insulted,'
the headteacher said.
And the girl said, 'Where do you
usually go?'**

I won a race yesterday.
I beat an egg.

Q. Who went too near the fire at Hogwarts?
A. Harry Hotter.

Mummy Bear said to Baby Bear, 'Stop moaning!'
And Baby Bear said, 'But I'm a little grizzly.'

I'm great at cooking omelettes. I make them **eggsactly** right.

We said to our science teacher, 'If frozen water is iced water, and frozen tea is iced tea, what do you call frozen ink?'
He said, 'Iced ink.'
We said, 'Yeah, we can smell it from here.'

Q. What goes round the world but stays in one corner?
A. A postage stamp.

Knock!
What do you mean, 'knock'? It's 'knock, knock'.
But I'm the knock-less monster.

Q. What's orange and
sounds like a parrot?
A. A carrot.

Q. Where do detectives live when
they're old?
A. Sherlock Homes.

Q. What did one eye say to the other?
A. There's something between us and
it smells.

Q. What did the scarf say to the hat?
A. I'll go round, you go on ahead.

Q. Who was keeping an eye on
everyone at Christmas?
A. A mince spy.

18

Q. What day of the week is it best to have fish and chips?
A. Fry-day.

19

Q. What do you call a fish with no eyes?
A. Fshhhhh.

Q. What do you call a boomerang that
doesn't come back?
A. A twig.

Q. What do you call a deer with no eyes?
A. No idea.

Q. What do you call a deer with no eyes
and no legs?
A. Still no idea.

Q. What do you call someone who's afraid of Santa?
A. Claus-trophobic.

Q. What goes on and on and has an eye in the middle?
A. An onion.

Q. What do you call a French man wearing beach sandals?
A. Philippe Faloppe.

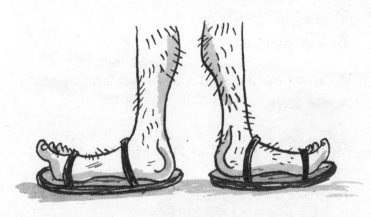

Q. How does the sea say hello?
A. It waves.

Q. What's the difference between a weasel and a stoat?
A. A weasel is weaselly recognized but a stoat is stoatally different.

Q. Why did the banana go to hospital?
A. It wasn't peeling well.

Q. Which shellfish are the strongest?
A. Mussels.

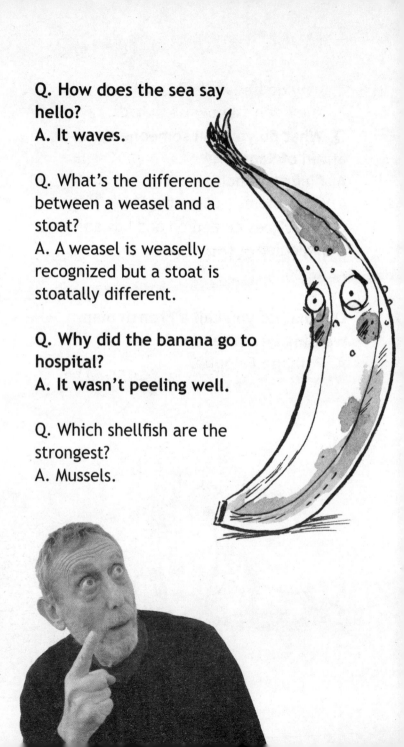

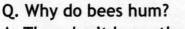

Q. Why do bees hum?
A. They don't know the words.

Q. Which goalkeeper can jump higher
than a crossbar?
A. All of them – a crossbar can't jump!

Knock, knock.
Who's there?
Cows.
Cows who?
No, they don't. Cows moo.

Try and do this:
Think of a number. Add 9. Take away 4.
Multiply it by 2. Add 5. Take away 3.
Shut your eyes.
It's dark, isn't it?

When Old Mother Hubbard got to the
cupboard she found that there was
nothing there. She said seven letters.
What seven letters?

O I C U R M T

**In the olden days, people
used to buy birds from
pet shops.
Quite often they
went cheap.**

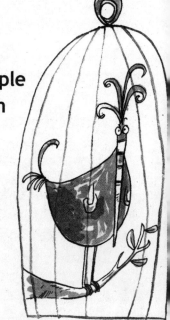

Q. What's worse than finding a maggot in your apple?
A. Finding half a maggot.

Q. Why did the mushroom get invited to all the parties?
A. 'Coz he's a fungi!

I was at a party and it was full of fungi. Not mushroom.

Q. What did Robin Hood say when the arrow just missed him?
A. That was an arrow escape.

DOCTOR, DOCTOR

Doctor, doctor, I feel like an iPad.
You won't need these tablets then.

Doctor, doctor, I feel like a million dollars.
Yes, I thought you looked green and wrinkled.

Doctor, doctor, people keep ignoring me.
Next!

27

Doctor, doctor, I feel like a pack of cards.
I'll deal with you later.

Doctor, doctor, I feel like a washing machine.
Don't worry, it's just something going round.

Doctor, doctor, I feel like a broken biscuit.
Crumbs!

Doctor, doctor, my sister thinks she's a lift.
Tell her to come in.
I can't. She doesn't stop at this floor.

Doctor, doctor, I feel like a needle.
I see your point.

Doctor, doctor, I think I'm a dog.
How long have you been feeling like this?
Ever since I was a puppy.

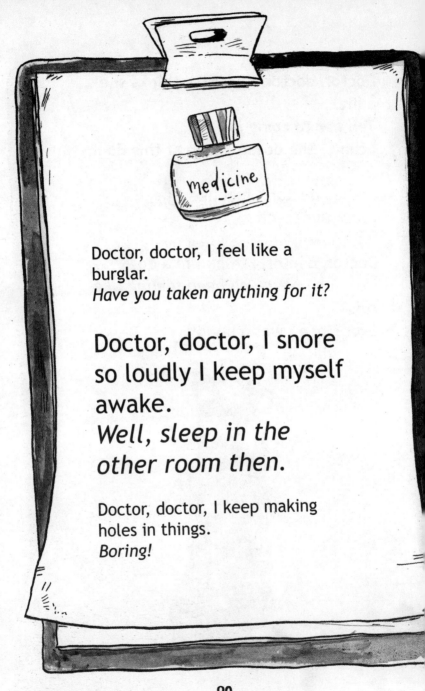

Doctor, doctor, I feel like a burglar.
Have you taken anything for it?

Doctor, doctor, I snore so loudly I keep myself awake.
Well, sleep in the other room then.

Doctor, doctor, I keep making holes in things.
Boring!

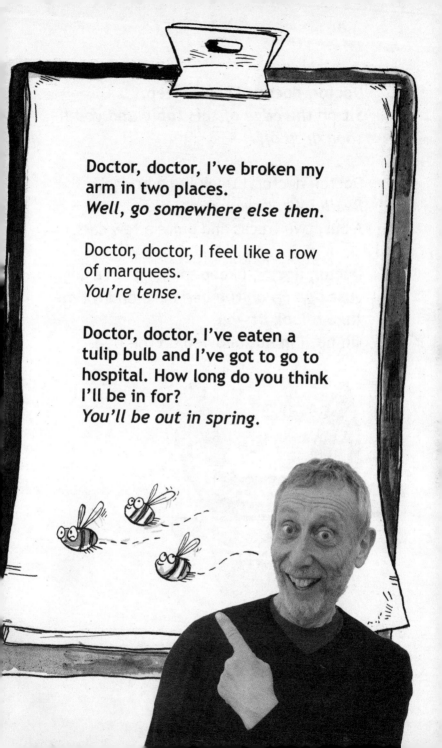

Doctor, doctor, I've broken my
arm in two places.
Well, go somewhere else then.

Doctor, doctor, I feel like a row
of marquees.
You're tense.

Doctor, doctor, I've eaten a
tulip bulb and I've got to go to
hospital. How long do you think
I'll be in for?
You'll be out in spring.

Doctor, doctor, I can't sleep.
Sit on the edge of this table and you'll soon drop off.

Doctor, doctor, I think I'm a bridge.
Really? What came over you?
A bus, two trucks and quite a few cars.

Doctor, doctor, I keep thinking I'm a dog.
Just pop up on the bed here and let me take a look at you.
Oh no, I'm not allowed on the bed.

32

Doctor, doctor, I feel like a chicken.
Well, stop it now.
But we like the eggs.

Doctor, doctor, I've got something awful
on my neck.
It's your head.

Doctor, doctor, I feel like a leek.
Well, don't do it here.

Doctor, doctor, I'd like to see Doctor
Vivvynivvywiffy.
Doctor who?
No, he's not a real doctor.

Doctor, doctor, I think I'm a bell.
Go home, have a rest and give me a ring later.

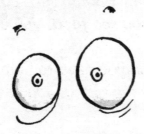

Doctor, doctor, what do you think of this eye?
It looks fine to me. And you've got another one that's just the same.

Doctor, doctor...
No, stop right there, I know what's wrong with you. You need a new pair of glasses.
How did you know?
You came in through the window.

Doctor, doctor, I've swallowed my pen.
Borrow mine.

Doctor, doctor, I keep putting on weight.
*Ah yes, you must be on the seafood
diet. When you see food, you eat it.*

Doctor, doctor, you have to help me out.
Just go the same way as you came in.

Doctor, doctor, I feel like a poodle.
You should see a dogtor.

Doctor, doctor, I feel like I'm in a hurdle race and I'm standing in front of a hurdle.
You'll get over it.

Doctor, doctor, I'm shrinking!
You'll just have to be a little patient.

Doctor, doctor, I feel like it's curtains for me.
Pull yourself together.

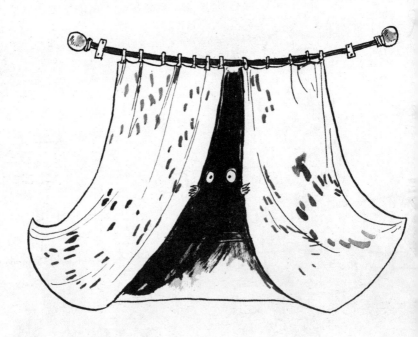

Q. Which girl in the class had eaten all the Quality Streets?
A. Chocolatey Claire.

Q. Why did 10 start getting worried?

A. Because 7, 8, 9.

Knock, knock.
Who's there?
Gnomey.
Gnomey who?
Don't you know me?

Q. Why did the scientist take the door bell off his front door?
A. So he could win the Nobel Prize.

A man I know was driving along the motorway.
His mobile phone rang.
It was his wife.
'Irving?' she says. 'Yes?' he says. 'You in the car?' she says. 'Yes,' he says. 'You driving?' she says. 'Yes,' he says. 'Irving, you on the motorway?' 'Yes,' he says. 'Irving, be careful!' she says, 'I'm watching the news. There's a crazy man on the motorway right now, driving the wrong way!' Irving looked up ahead. 'Not just one, darling. There's hundreds! Hundreds and hundreds of them!'

Q. Why was the archaeologist upset?
A. His job was in ruins.

Q. What do you call a teacher who's always late?
A. Mr Bus.

A friend of mine had an emergency.
There was a fire in his house. He rang the fire service.
'There's a fire in my house.'
'Stay calm, sir,' said the person on the switchboard. 'Can you tell me how we get to your place?'
And my friend said, 'Don't you guys still have those big red trucks?'

Q. What do you call
a cow eating grass?
A. A lawn-mooer.

Q. What's the biggest ant?
A. An eleph-ant.

A girl I know got lost in the woods.
She called out, 'Can anyone help me?'
A voice came from inside her rucksack.
'I'm your calculator. You can count
on me.'

**Q. How do you say the alphabet
backwards?**

A. **T, E, B, A, H, P, L, A, E, H, T.**

Q. How do you start a teddy bear race?
A. Ready, teddy, go.

Q. How do you start a goat race?
A. Ready, steady, goat!

43

Q. How do you start a plant race?
A. Ready, steady, grow!

Q. How do you start a firefly race?
A. Ready, steady, glow.

Q. How do you start a jelly race?
A. Get set.

Q. What's the difference between a bottle of medicine and a doormat?
A. One's shaken up and taken and the other's taken up and shaken.

Q. **Where do frogs leave their bags?**
A. **In the croakroom.**

Q. What's the opposite of hieroglyphs?
A. Loweroglyphs.

A famous spider was talking to her fans:
'And if you want to know more about what I'm doing, go to my website.'

I've heard they're going to improve badminton.
They're calling it goodminton.

Q. How did the football pitch end up as a triangle?
A. Someone took a corner.

Q. Why was the defender fed up?
A. He was left back in the changing room.

Q. What do you call someone who kicks leaves?
A. Russell.

Q. What do you call someone with a spade on his head?
A. Doug.

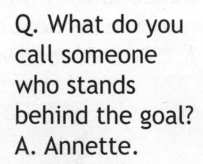

Q. What do you call someone who stands behind the goal?
A. Annette.

Q. What do you call someone with a bit of wood on his head?
A. Edward.

Q. What do you call someone with two bits of wood on his head?
A. Edward Wood.

Q. What do you call someone with three bits of wood on his head?
A. Edward Woodward.

Q. What do earwigs sing at football matches?
A. Earwig-o! Earwig-o! Earwig-o!

Two dads ran in the fathers' race on sports day.
One ran in short bursts, the other ran in burst shorts.

Q. What's the best day to buy chewing gum?
A. Tuesday.

Dad, what's the capital of France?
Sorry, son, I don't know.
Dad, how far is it to the moon?
Sorry, son, I don't know.
Dad, what's the longest word in the
dictionary?
Sorry, son, I don't know.
You don't mind me asking these
questions, do you Dad?
*Of course not, son. Asking questions is
how you learn things.*

Dad, why do you keep rubbing the top
of your head and winking?
To keep the tigers away, son.
But there aren't any tigers round here,
Dad.
See, son, it works.

Dad dashed out the flat on the
27th floor and told the boys,
Mikey and Ikey, to be good.
When he got out of the lift at
the bottom he remembered
he had left the car key in
the flat.
He called up to the boys.
Ikey put his head out the
window.
'Ikey!' he shouted, 'Throw my
key out the window!'
And Ikey threw Mikey out the
window.

A little boy couldn't face going into school. His mum and dad went to work, and he secretly stayed at home.

He rang the school.

He put on a very deep voice and said, 'I'm very sorry but Alfie won't be at school today.'

'Oh yes,' said the school secretary, 'and who's speaking?'

'My dad,' said Alfie.

Dr Spooner was a teacher at Oxford
University but he muddled up the first
letters in what he was saying.
So instead of saying, 'That's a well-
oiled bicycle', he said 'That's a well-
boiled icicle.'
One day he was angry that one of the
students had been doing nothing for
most of the year.
He said, 'Mr Jarvis, you've tasted two
whole worms.'

Q. Where were the general's armies?
A. Up his sleevies.

Q. What's the opposite of cock-a-doodle-do?
A. Cock-a-doodle-don't.

Q. What's green and has wheels?
A. Grass – sorry I lied about the wheels.

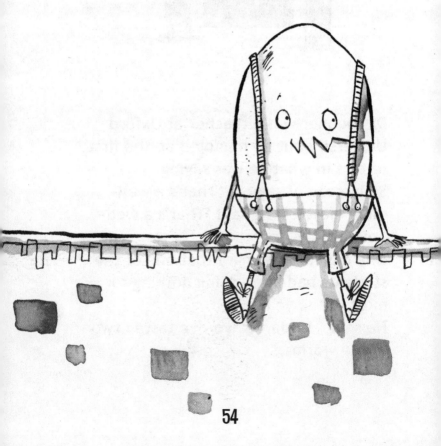

Humpty Dumpty
sat on the wall.
Humpty Dumpty
had a great fall.
All the king's horses
and all the king's men
trod on him.

Q. Why is an elephant huge, grey and wrinkled?
A. Because if it was small, white and smooth it would be a pill.

Q. What did ancient Britons say when they saw the Romans arriving?
A. Here come the Romans.

Q. Why were the little plants singing 'Humpty Dumpty'?
A. They were in the nursery.

I know a couple who had a child who didn't talk. Of course he didn't talk when he was just born, but he didn't start talking when most children start. When he was three he still hadn't said a word. Same at four. Then one day the family were sitting round the table having their lunch and the little boy looked up, shook his head and said, 'No, too salty!' Everyone looked at him. 'That's amazing!' said his mum, 'that's amazing. But... but... why didn't you talk before?' And the little boy said, 'Well, the food's been fine up 'til now.'

Waiter, waiter, what's this fly
doing in my soup?
Front crawl, sir.

Waiter, waiter, there are
two flies in my bowl of
soup and they look like
they're playing football!
*Well, sir, let's hope they
play better next week –
they're in the cup.*

Waiter, waiter, there's a fly in
my soup.
*Don't worry, sir, it won't drink
much.*

Waiter, waiter, I'm looking at the
menu, I can't see spaghetti on it.
*There it is sir, down the bottom.
I'll wipe it off for you right away.*

Waiter, waiter, will my pizza be long?
No, sir, it'll be round.

Waiter, waiter, can I have burnt toast,
mouldy cheese and water in a dirty glass?
*No, sir, we don't serve that sort of
thing in this restaurant.*
That's funny, it's what you gave me
yesterday.

Waiter: Now, sir, 'today's special...'
Customer: Indeed, waiter, and so is every day.

Waiter, waiter, what's this?
It's bean soup.
I don't care what it used to be, what sort of soup is it now?

Waiter, waiter, I'm not eating this soup.
Why not, sir?
I haven't got a spoon.

Waiter, waiter, this egg is off.
Not my fault, sir, I only lay the tables.

Rudolph hadn't met the other reindeer
before and he was out with his mummy.
Up ahead of them messing about in
the snow were Prancer, Vixen, Comet,
Cupid, Donner and Blitzen, but all
Rudolph could see was a cloud of snow.
'Mummy,' said Rudolph, 'what's that?'
She looked up at the sky.
'Looks like rain, dear.'

The children were going for a walk in the
woods to find out all about nature.
'There's a robin,' said the teacher.
They walked on some more.
'There's an oak tree,' said the teacher.
'Now, who knows what that brown wrinkly
stuff is on the trunk of the oak tree?'
No one knew.
'Come on, everyone. What is it?'
No one knew.
'Bark,' said the teacher.
And one boy went, 'Woof!'

There were two eggs being boiled.

'Phew!' said one, 'it isn't half getting hot.'

'Too right,' said the other, 'but if you think that's bad, when we get out of here, they'll bash you over the head with a spoon.'

I know an old bloke,
his name is Lord Jim.
He's got a wife
who throws tomatoes at him.
Now, tomatoes are juicy,
don't injure the skin.
But these ones they did:
they were inside a tin.

Q. What did the dog say to its bone?
A. It's been nice gnawing you.

I saw a dog the other day. It was looking
at a sign saying 'Wet paint.'
Then it did.

Q. What's Usain Bolt's favourite meal?
A. Fast food.

My cat is very intelligent. When I'm watching videos, she knows how to press '**paws**'.

Why do they put those signs up in
supermarkets that say, 'NO DOGS!'?
*It's because they don't want dogs in
a place where there's food.*
But dogs can't read.

Q. What shape looks like a dead parrot?
A. A polygon.

I've got a very long word here and I'm
going to ask you how to spell it.
But I already know.
Really? Go on then.

I,T.

Q. Do you know why the mummy who was in a tomb in the pyramid for thousands of years never spoke?
A. It was too wrapped up in itself.

Q. Do you know what the great boy king of ancient Egypt said when they knocked on the door of his tomb?
A. Toot! And come in.

Q. What game do little pharaohs play in their tombs in the pyramids?
A. Mummies and deadies.

Q. What's a crocodile's favourite game?
A. Snap.

There's a French cheese that seems very friendly. It's called 'Come in, Bert.'

There is a winding passage
that goes up to my heart,
and what comes down this passage
is commonly called a fart.
The fart is very useful,
it sets the mind at ease.
It warms the bed on wintry nights
and disinfects the fleas.

Two little boys were playing.
One of them put a helmet on his head.
The other one said, 'Viking?'
And the boy with the helmet said,
'Vy not?'

Q. Where do cows go on holiday?
A. Moo York.

Q. How do cows add up?
A. On a cowculator.

Mum, I've been stung by a wasp.
Quick, let's put some cream on it.
Don't be daft, it's flown off now.

Why don't you go outside and play
football with your brother?
*Oh no, Mum, I'd much rather play
football with a ball.*

Q. What football team would you find in
an ice-cream van?
A. Aston Vanilla.

I went to the doctor and he says I can't play football.
Oh, he's seen you play, then.

The world's greatest goalkeeper
was **Robbie "Saves" O'Riley**.
One day he was walking down
the street and a woman
recognized him.
She turned to her friend and said,
'That's "Saves"!'
'Oh really?'
'No, O'Riley.'

Q. Why was Cinderella thrown out of the football team?
A. She kept running away from the ball.

Q. What's the difference between a gutter and a bad goalkeeper?
A. One catches drops, the other drops catches.

Oh dear, you've got your shoes on the wrong feet.
But they're the only feet I've got.

Hey, look at you, you're wearing one red sock and one blue sock.
I know, and I've got another pair just like it at home.

Q. What do you call a woman wearing a black hat, riding on a broom, with a slice of bread on each ear?
A. A sand-witch.

Did you see that you can do sunbathing as an Olympic sport now?
Are you going to go in for it?
No, I'll only get bronze.

Q. What do William the Conqueror and Winnie the Pooh have in common?
A. Their middle name.

Q. When did Charles I reign?
A. When it was cloudy.

Q. What's the hairiest tree in the forest?
A. The fir tree.

Teacher: Why is your homework in your mother's handwriting?
Pupil: I used her pen.

Q. What do you call a cockerel who wakes you up every morning?
A. An alarm cluck.

Q. Why did the traffic light go red?
A. It had to change in the middle of the street.

78

I've got some secret butter.
Go on, tell me about it.
No, you might spread it.

Q. What did the dog say when its tail got stuck in the door?
A. It won't be long now.

Q. What's the name of the film about dinosaurs and pigs?
A. Jurassic Pork.

Once upon a time, a monster was eating a comedian.
All of a sudden, the monster spat him out on to his plate.
'What's the matter?' said the monster's mum, 'don't you like it?'
'No,' said the monster, 'it tastes funny.'

Q. What do cats eat for breakfast?
A. Mice Krispies.

Q. Why was the piano outside the house?
A. It had lost its keys.

Q. Why did the ocean roar?
**A. There were crabs crawling all over
its bottom.**

Have you seen the salad dressing?
No, I was in the other room.

Two snakes were sitting on a
park bench.
One snake said to the other,
'Are we the kind of snake that
coils round people and squeezes
them to death, or are we the
poisonous kind?'
The other snake said, 'We're
the kind of snake that coils
round people and squeezes
them to death.'
'That's good,' said the first
snake.
'Why's that?' said the second.
'I just bit my lip.'

Q. What do you call an elephant at the North Pole?
A. Lost.

Q. Who makes a living from driving customers away?
A. A taxi driver.

Q. In one old film, a cowboy rode into town on Friday, stayed for three days, then rode home on Friday. How was this possible?
A. His horse was called Friday.

Q. What has a bottom at the top?
A. Your legs.

Q. Which weighs more, a ton of feathers or a ton of bricks?
A. They both weigh the same – a ton.

One-one was a race horse.
Two-two was one, too.
One-one won one race.
Two-two won one, too.

I had a wooden whistle but it wouldn't whistle.

Q. What's at the end of everything?
A. G

How would you describe the rain in this part of the country?

Little drops of water falling out of the sky all at the same time.

I was sitting by a pond one day and I heard a little creature by the water telling a story about how his car had broken down.
'Well, the AA came, hooked me up to their car and brought me all the way back, right up to my front door. I walked in and my friend was there. My friend looked up and said, 'Toad!' and I said, 'Yes, all the way home.'

When I was a wee-wee tot,
they took me from my wee-wee cot.
They put me on my wee-wee pot,
to see if I would wee or not.
When they found that I would not,
they took me from my wee-wee pot,
they put me in my wee-wee cot,
where I wee-wee quite a lot.

Did you just pick your nose?
No, it's the one I was born with.

The perfume shop was waiting for a box
of new perfumes to arrive. When they
were delivered, the owner of the shop
opened up the box, opened some
of the bottles and squirted them
– no perfume smell at all. It
was a load of non-scents.

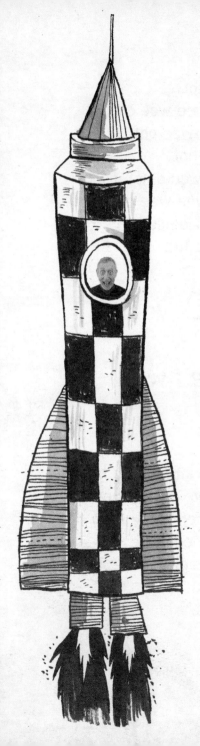

The rocket was taking off, and one astronaut was hungry. He looked at the clock. It was midday. He turned to the others and said, 'What are we having for launch?'

One neighbour was talking to the other:

Hey, didn't you hear me banging on your wall last night?
No, we were making too much noise to hear anything like that.

Roses are red, violets are blue. Most poems rhyme. This one doesn't.

When's your birthday?
Every year.
When were you born?
On my birthday.

Pete and Re-Pete were in the room. Pete got up and went out. Who was left?

Re-Pete.

Pete and Re-Pete were in the room. Pete got up and went out. Who was left?

Re-Pete.

Pete and Re-Pete were in the room. Pete got up and went out. Who was left?

Re-Pete.

Pete and Re-Pete were in the room. Pete got up and went out. Who was left?

Re-Pete.

Pete and Re-Pete were in the room. Pete got up and went out. Who was left?

Re-Pete.

Pete and Re-Pete were in the room. Pete got up and went out. Who was left?

Re-Pete.

Pete and Re-Pete were in the

It was the Insects vs Little Beasties cup final. An incredibly exciting match. Insects were winning 2–nil, right up to the last five minutes. Then Little Beasties took off Snail and brought on Centipede. It made a fantastic difference. Centipede scored three times in the last few minutes of the game and Little Beasties won the cup.

After the match, the players were sitting round having their after-match meal and the captain of Insects, Bee, said to Woodlouse, captain of Little Beasties, 'How come you left it so late to bring on Centipede?'

'He was putting on his boots.'

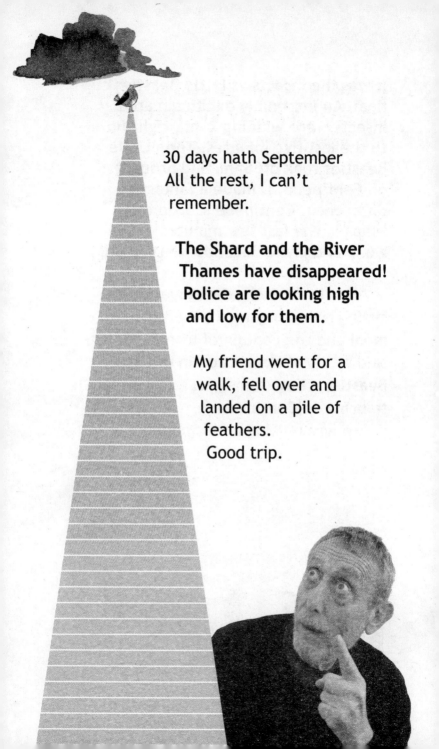

30 days hath September
All the rest, I can't
remember.

**The Shard and the River
Thames have disappeared!
Police are looking high
and low for them.**

My friend went for a
walk, fell over and
landed on a pile of
feathers.
Good trip.

An author came to the school
and gave a really interesting
talk about her book, *Silly Solly*.
Everyone laughed. They loved
Silly Solly.
At the end of the talk, she
said, 'Now, has anyone got any
questions?'
One boy put his hand up.
'Yes?' said the author.
'Who won the FA Cup in 1985?'

Q. What was the omelette race like?
A. Eggciting!

A couple were looking to buy a flat. The woman looked out the window. 'Is it quiet here?' she asked.
'Yes, absolutely,' said the man selling the flat, 'totally quiet, except when the people round here are noisy.'

I bet you can't repeat seven words I say.
OK, go on then.
I am a total doughnut.
I am a total doughnut.
Wrong!
What do you mean,
'wrong'? I repeated exactly
what you said.
No you didn't. I said five words: 'I am a
total doughnut.' Then I said, 'Wrong!'
and you said, 'What do you mean,
'wrong'?'

Mum, I'm going to the barbers. How do
you think I should have my hair?
On your head, I think.

Q. What letter keeps you waiting?
A. Q

How do you write 'endless love'?

L, O, V.

Q. What's R.P.I.?
A. A grave error.

Q. What does this say?

NOPPPLEE

A. No peas please. (NO Ps PL Es)

Q. Which three letters make the world go round.

A. **N, R, G**.

Q. Which two letters wish they were like the others?
A. N, V.

Q. Why are you only friends with 25 of the letters in the alphabet?
A. Because I hate U.

If you leave Alphabetti Spaghetti on the stove and go out, it could spell disaster.

I can never remember how to get to the very end of the alphabet. I don't know Y.

Q. Why can't pirates say the alphabet?
A. They get lost at C.

Q. What's the quickest way to count to a
hundred.
A. One, two
leave a few
ninety-nine, a hundred.

Beans, beans, good for your heart,
The more you eat, the more you fart.
The more you fart, the better you feel,
so eat baked beans for every meal.

Well, Goldilocks, you've been a long time at the shops, where have you been?

There was this house and some chairs and I had some porridge, and then I went to bed and when I woke up there were some bears and there was a little one that was moaning about me being there...

Goldilocks, I've told you before, don't make up stories.

They've
discovered
a dinosaur
that looks like a
doormat.
Flat-on-the-floor-us.

Q. How do you catch a rabbit?
A. Hide in a bush and look like a lettuce.

Q. How do you play the piano after
you've had cod and chips?
A. With fish fingers.

Q. What do you call the game where you
throw furniture at each other?
A. Table tennis.

Knock, knock.
Who's there?
The Interrupting Cow.
The Interrupt—
MOOOOO!

A farmer and his friend were walking past the farmer's horse when the horse looked up and said, 'I won the Grand National, you know.'

'Wow!' said the farmer's friend, 'was that your horse talking? Incredible.'

'Oh, it's not true. He only came in second.'

We were driving through the countryside, and we suddenly saw a three-legged sheep, so I got out the car and knocked on the farmer's door.

'I'm very sorry,' I said, 'but I see that you've got a three-legged sheep there. I don't want to be nosy, but how come?'

'Ah, yes,' said the farmer, 'that's an amazing sheep that one. Do you know, one time we were away from the farm and a fire broke out in the barn, and that sheep ran into the house – we leave the door open – rang for the fire brigade and they came and put the fire out.'

'Mmmm,' I said, 'but what about the – you know – the three legs?'

'Ah well,' said the farmer, 'that's an amazing sheep that one. One time, we were away from the farm, and old Joe here, he collapsed in the field, and that sheep ran into the house – we leave the door open – rang for the ambulance and they came and took old Joe to the hospital, and he's as right as rain now.'

'Mmmm,' I said, 'but what about the –

you know – the three legs?'

'Ah well,' said the farmer, 'that's an amazing sheep that one. One time, we were away from the farm, and that sheep spotted some burglars snooping round the back of the house and, what with the door being open, that sheep nipped into the house, rang for the police and they were over really fast, picked up the burglars and they're in prison now.'

'Mmm,' I said, 'but the – you know – the three legs?'

'Well,' said the farmer, 'with a sheep like that you don't want to eat it all at once, do you?'

A man walked into a shop and said,
'I need a plug.'
'Yes, sir,' said the woman behind the
counter, 'Gulp backwards.'

Nothing rhymes with nothing.

I didn't mean to reverse my car over
my laptop.
I was backing up.

Mummy Goat waved
goodbye to Little Goat.
'You're on your own,
kid.'

Q. What happened to the boy who sat on the radiator?
A. He got a hot cross bum.

Q. How good do you think the ancient Romans were at school?
A. Well, they could do Latin.

I took a picture of myself making a cake.
Selfie raising flour.

My dog's done one on the floor and now there's a poodle piddle puddle.

Q. How do writers get wax out of their ears?
A. They work it out with a pencil.

'The thing is,' my dad was saying, 'the thing is, when I was a boy...'
And I said, 'You've told me this story before and...'
And he said, 'But the thing is, what I haven't told you is...'
And I said, 'Could you please not talk when I'm interrupting?'

I was scared stiff the other day. I thought I saw a shark in my bedroom. I reckoned it was in my chest of jaws.

Have you seen that movie where these great big letters turn up and start destroying everything? It's called *War of the Words*.

I love all the latest pop music, but my favourite is indie stuff. A bit alternative... like The Other Direction.

My favourite band sings about making fires in the olden days: Coalplay.

Q. What do you call a popstar who swears?
A. Justin Bleeper.

In one of the 007 films, you weren't allowed to see most of it. It was called *James Banned*.

Q. What do snowmen sing at birthday parties?
A. Freeze a jolly good fellow...

I was in a school and I did my poem that goes:

'Down behind the dustbin
I met a dog called Jim.
He didn't know me
and I didn't know him.'

and a boy shouted out,
'Well how did you know his name was Jim, then?'

I was on a bus and a boy said,
'Are you Michael Rosen?' I said, 'Yes.'
And he said, 'You look just like him.'

The last movie I saw, I just can't get it out of my mind.
Cling Film.

Q. Why did the hipster burn his tongue?
A. Because he drank his coffee before it was cool.

Q. What's brown and sounds like a bell?
A. Dung.

Q. What did Bruno say when he went to Mars?
A. 'Don't believe me, just watch.'

Q. What's faster, hot or cold?
A. Hot, because you can catch a cold.

In one old story there's a little boy who gets some beans and they're so magical they tell him where the treasure is: Jack and the Beans Talk.

Q. What's brown and sticky?
A. A stick.

THE SWORD FIGHT THAT WENT WRONG
BY IVAN EAROFF

THE WORST JOURNEY EVER
a book dedicated to Helen Backagain

Wet Clothes by I.P. Inthewind

FELL OFF A CLIFF
by Eileen Dover

Who Had the Cakes? Adam Addem

THE WARM ROOM
BY RAY D. AYTER

Singalong
by Carry O'Kee

ACROSS THE DESERT
by Rhoda Camel

SOMEWHERE TO KEEP YOUR CLOTHES
BY CHESTER DRAWS

Watching Rivers
by Flo Quick

THE ENDS OF MY BODY
BY HANS ERNFEET

Pleased to Meet You by Heidi High

GOT THERE IN THE END
BY JUSTIN TIME

Dancing Outfit
by Leah Tard

THE HOLE IN THE ROOF by Lee King

SAYING IT LOUDER
by M. Fersiss

Doing an Odd Thing
by Major Look

A MISTAKE by Mark Trong

KUNG-FU, KARATE AND JUDO
BY MARSHA LARTS

My Gran Looks On
by Nancy Sittall

Take a Rest by Neil Down

THE TIP-TAP COOKBOOK
by Pat Acayke

Absolutely Gorgeous
by Ravi Shing

MORNING CHECK
by Reggie Stir

Clean Glasses by Seymour Clearly

Awful Jokes by Terry Bull

THE TRUTH
BY TERESA GREEN

WHAT COLOUR IS YOUR FURNITURE?
Ebenezer Blackwood

The Sound
of Autumn
Russell Inleaves

Standing for Too Long by Sid Down

SITTING DOWN FOR TOO LONG
by Stan Dupp

LISTEN TO ME BY MARK MYWORDS

GREAT SPEECHES
by Toby or Nott-Toby

SO UNFAIR by Y. Me

Tea Please!
by Phil McCupp

Take Away by Will Order

STRAIGHTENING THE DUVET
BY ANITA BEDD

The Broken Window
by Eva Brick

WILL HE WIN?
BY BETTY WONT

A Great Australian Building
by Sidney Oprahouse

NIGHTWEAR by P. Jarmers

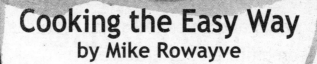
Cooking the Easy Way
by Mike Rowayve

About the author

Michael Rosen is one of the UK's most well-loved contemporary poets and children's fiction writers.

Born in London in 1946, he started writing poetry at the age of 12 and is now one of the most renowned figures in the children's book world.

In his career so far, he's won numerous awards – including the Smarties Book Prize for his classic picture book, *We're Going On A Bear Hunt* – and was the Children's Laureate between 2007 and 2009.

Michael frequently appears on the radio and gives talks and lectures on children's literature.